Sammy

Learns His

A B C

DEDICATED TO

This book is dedicated to all children because they deserve to have an excellent introduction to learning.

Sammy Learns

His

A B C

by

Samuel Browne

Sammy Learns His ABC by Samuel Browne

Published by NGOWE
www.ngowe.com

Tampa, FL 33611

1st Edition: 2016

ISBN: 978-0-9983204-3-4

Illustrated by
Bassey B. Inyang

Charles E. Chukukere

ACKNOWLEDGEMENTS

The Author wishes to thank God for blessing him with wonderful encouraging parents because they inspire him to aim high, achieve beyond all expectations, think outside the box, and to aim to the sky. They also teach and encourage him to move beyond his today and think about his tomorrow; that success lies with him, but he has to reach out and grab it. He would like to thank his past teachers at Reading Rainbow USVI, Surefoot International School, Calabar, Nigeria, and Robinson High School Tampa Florida.

INTRODUCTION

Sammy Learns His ABC by Samuel Browne is the first book from the Sammy Series which takes you on a journey of how Sammy learned to read by the age of three. This book supports learning that drives through thoughtful planning, careful application of basic principles, and repetition combination with love and many kisses. These are essential ingredients needed to encourage young minds to thirst for more of the unknown. Even though the author was only 15 years when he did this book he wants to share his experience so that others can be inspired to do the same. Join him and become an agent for change. Enjoy!

One bright and
sunny day,
Sammy woke up
and guess what he asked?
"Mommy, Mommy
can I sing my

ABC?

It is my most favorite song of all."
Mommy smiled and said,
"Yes, you can start
right now."

And so Mommy and Sammy played with his blocks while he sang his **A B C**.

A B C D

E F G H

I J K L

M N O P

Q R S T

U V W X

Y Z

"Since you know your A B C, can you go around the house and label everything you know from
A to Z?" She asked.
"Ok!" Sammy said excitedly.
"I found it!" He said.

" A is for Apple,

B is for Banana,

C is for the cat." He said as his little cat walked into the room.

" D is for the dog;

E is for…? E is for…...?" He paused.

"Mommy there is nothing that begins with E in the house," Sammy said sadly.

"Are you sure? Look in your toy chest again." She replies. Sammy shouted as he ran back from his toy chest.

"**E** is for elephant,

F is for a frog,

G is for goat,

H is for…...oh no I can't find anything that begins with "h" in here," he says.

"Try elsewhere." she replies. Sammy moved around the house and on his bed guess what he found?

"**H** is for my horse!" he said as he picked up his toy horse on the bed.

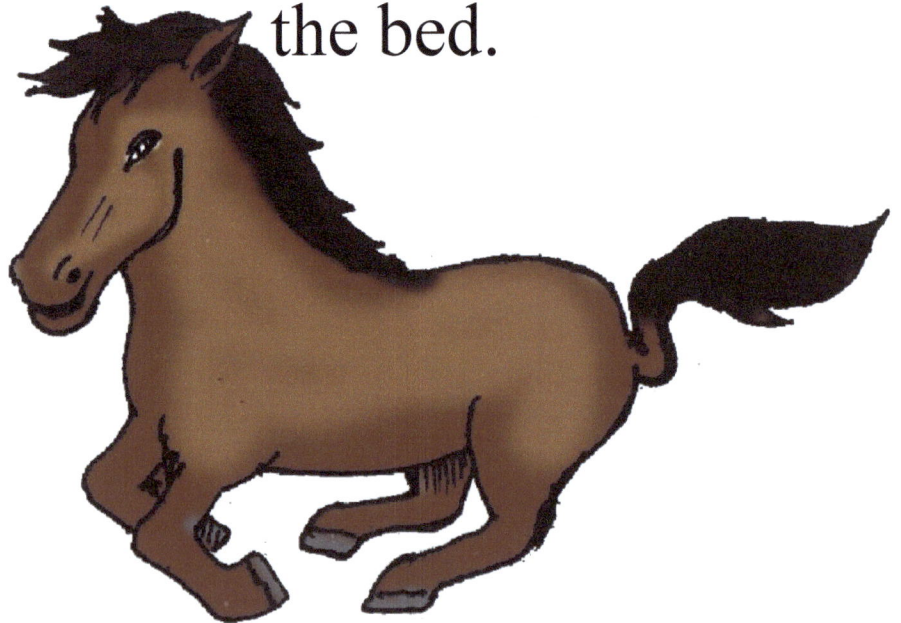

"I is for ice-cream!"

he exclaimed as he looked
in the refrigerator

"And **J** is for jug!"

He shouted happily!

"You have done well so far Sammy but what starts with K?" asked Mom as she kissed him lovingly.

"Well that's easy, Kite like the one daddy and I fly," Sammy replied.

"K is for Kite,

L is for Lamp!" As he pointed at his lamp on the night table.

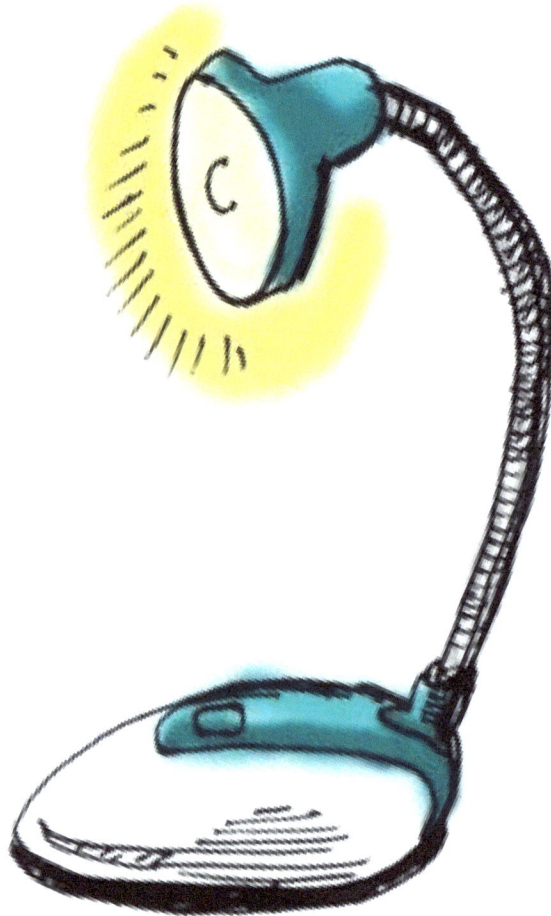

"M is for me, and

N is for my nose,

O is for …" Sammy runs into the kitchen "O is for orange,

P is for pot,

"Q is for ...." Sammy runs into his mother's bedroom. "Q is for Queen!"

As he jumps up and down on the bed.

"**R** is for rabbit MOMMY,

THERE IT GOES

HOPPING BY!!!

S is for

a snake in the grass,

T is for Toy!"
As he pulled some toys
from his toy chest.

"U is for this umbrella,

and  is

for my van!"

Sammy said quite proudly.

"W is for?" Asked Sammy's

"W" Mommy.

is for my watch."

As he looked at his wrist.

"X is for my xylophone,

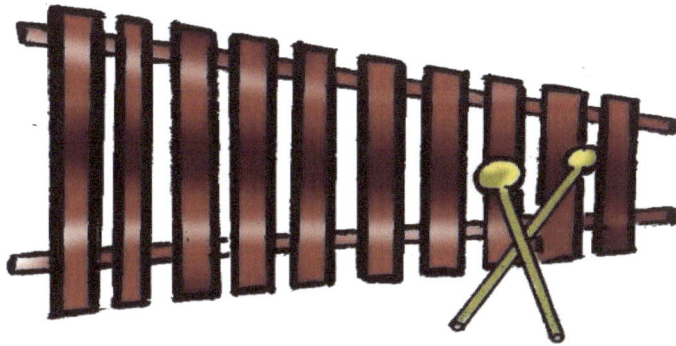

Y is for this yoyo,

and the last is **Z** for zebra!" he shouts as he picks up his toy zebra from off the chair.

"YEAH, I did my A B C."

"Well done Sammy, you look quite tired, go to bed and get some sleep." Mommy said.

"Ok Mommy," Sammy says as he heads up to bed to catch some ZZZ's

Author's Biography

Samuel Browne was born in 1999 in Atlanta Georgia but grew up on the beautiful island of St. Croix United States Virgin Island. He grew up an active child involved in soccer, basketball, baseball, tennis, and track and field. However, soccer was his main passion. He is an amazing soccer player and hopes that one day he is discovered by the national soccer team. He currently attends college and played for the Tampa Bay United U17 Soccer team. At present, his primary interests are education, writing poetry and songs, playing his piano, developing video games, and of course playing soccer. His ambition in life is to be the best he could be and to become an inspiration to others.

MORE BOOKS FROM THE SAMMY SERIES

Sammy Learns To Read At 3

Sammy Please Wash Your Hands

OTHER NGOWE BOOKS

Life To Me

The Sketcher

Melissa Against The World

www.ingramcontent.com/pod-product-compliance
Lightning Source LLC
Chambersburg PA
CBHW041553040426

42447CB00002B/164